I0488545

How to Make $10,000

Monthly

With

YouTube Videos

1

CHAPTER 1

Building YouTube Empire

1.   YouTube Account Creation:

The first action step to making your first million dollars is to create an account on YouTube. You can visit https://www.YouTube.com/account. Thereafter, you create channels for your videos base on your niche. The niche could be how to make money videos, natural remedies for some ailments, beauty tips etc.

After creating your channel, write the channel description of your channel according to your niche and then verify the channel through your phone number, you can start uploading your videos. Please note that you have to monetize your videos so that you can start earning immediately.

2.   AdSense Account Opening:

Before you start earning, visit https://www.google.com/adSense to link your YouTube account with your AdSense account for processing all your earnings and payments.

Note that YouTube pays its video publishers through AdSense which is a percentage of advertising and subscription revenues. AdSense can pay you via check, wire transfer or direct deposit.

3.   Channel Niche and Keywords:

To generate reasonable views on your channel, you must tie your niche to their keywords. The keywords enhances your chances of being noticed by search engines. Name your channel, choose channel icon, upload your channel art, and write your channel description according to your niche. You can setup featured, enable views and discussion. Do not forget to upload channel trailer, add sections to organize your channel and customize it.

CHAPTER 2

HOW TO CREATE YOUR VIDEOS

1. **Creative Common cc:** This enables you to get videos you can freely re-use and is readily available on the YouTube features. These are videos uploaded to YouTube which can be recycled for future use. There is no limit to the number of videos you can produce. You can also learn more of this on YouTube Community.

2. **Creative Studio:** This is a utility or feature on YouTube that is used to produce videos manually with the use of picture that relates with your niche of your interest. On this utility, which is a tab on YouTube website, you can create the following:

(a.) Video with music
(b.) Video with screen shots and labels
(c.) Video with free music without license

3. **CamStudio:** This is a software that you can download from CamStudio website that can be used to capture desktop presentations, other peoples video on the web etc. It also has a utility that will enable you to upload it to your YouTube account legally. You can use this utility to also capture videos on YouTube which are your niche category and upload to your YouTube account legally.

CHAPTER 3

HOW TO USE TITTLES, DESCRIPTIONS AND TAGS

1. **Tittles:** This is the first field on the box when you are uploading your video. That is the name your video should be called. The right way to use it is to make sure that the search criteria for the video is at the right hand side of the tittle e.g How to make money with YouTube videos, make sure the tittles well punctuated.

2. **Description:** This is the second field on the YouTube box when uploading your videos. That is where you describe the content of your video, it must contain same reference in the tittle to make your video accessible, reachable and available in the search engine. For example, with the tittle above, the description should be "How to make money with YouTube video with secrets. Note that money, YouTube videos and Secrets are also in the tittle.

3. **Tags:** This is the third field on the YouTube box when uploading your videos. That is where you name your video different names with reference to the tittle and description. For example, from your video, tittle and description, our tags should be: YouTube, YouTube videos, videos, make money, money secrets etc. Those names must be separated by commas.

CHAPTER 4

HOW TO USE PLAYLISTS TO INCREASE AND REVENUE

Playlists are created through the video manager on the YouTube. It is a process of linking your videos together as they are related to each other according to the niche. Note that if linked, when a video is played, other videos with be activate and show up and play immediately the first video finishes playing leading to multiple views which translates to more revenue. You can also ride on other popular videos by tying your videos to them through playlists to increase your views. Your videos plays immediately the popular video finishes playing. You video acts like a parasite getting views through other videos and increase revenue and views geometrically.

You can have as many playlist as possible depending on the number of your videos. You can also submit your playlist links and embed them on your sites and social media. The playlist will help your videos to attract more views which will definitely convert to more revenue from Google AdSense. The playlist could be in different niche like insurance, education, entertainment, love, games, minecraft, wrestling, apps, etc. The more playlist you have the more the chance of your videos being discovered by search engines.

CHAPTER 5

HOW TO USE THUMNAILS AND SUBSCRIBERS BOX TO ATTRACT VIEWS

THUMBNAILS:

These are displayed on your videos showing what information your video has for its audience. The more attractive the thumbnail is the more the video gets views. The thumbnails can ne be replaced or changed with a better thumbnail which could be a picture of the video. The thumbnail should be well fashioned to give beauty, relevance, and creative representation of the video. Note that the more views your video attracts the more revenue you make, therefore, create a beautiful thumbnail.

Your video thumbnail must be attractive so as to attract views, the more attractive your thumbnails are the more clicks you get should will convert to revenue. Ensure that the thumbnails are beautifully added.

SUBSCRIBERS BOX:

This is a box below your video where viewers can click to subscribe to your channel. To get more viewers can click to subscribe, there must be deliberate plan for a call to action request on your subscription box for viewers to subscribe to your video. Setup a subscription link for your channel and embed it on your subscription box. Note the more subscribers you have, the more views your videos get at announces to all of them whenever a new video is uploaded. Note that the more views your videos get, the more revenue you earn.

You can rinse and repeat. If the instructions are properly read and followed, you will be smiling to the bank in no distant time.

Mores so, do not forget to read all terms and conditions carefully. This is very important to prevent your account from being banned.

CHAPTER SIX

GETTING MORE VIEWS

Many people have become well-known, or even famous, because of their YouTube videos. But for every YouTube celebrity, there are thousands of people who have trouble getting views. If you want to get more views on your YouTube videos, then you have to not only make an amazing video, but you also have to know how to describe and share your creation. Using good descriptions, sharing your video with tons of people, and making sure your video looks great are a few ways to propel your video into the YouTube stratosphere.

APPROPRIATE DESCRIPTIONS

Name your video file accurately. If it's about a lizard, then the word "lizard" should be in the file name of the video. You can name it "scary-lizard.mov."

Give your video an appealing title. It should be short, engaging, and to the point. If your video is about your kid spilling macaroni and cheese everywhere, just call it "Mac and Cheese Disaster." It should pique your viewers' interests without giving too much away.

Describe your video thoroughly. Most people ignore this step, but you should take it seriously to increase your views. Describe your video as accurately as possible in the space you are given, taking 2-3 paragraphs to write an interesting and precise description of what people can expect when they see the video.

Use the best tags. Use all of the keywords from your title and description in the "tags" section to get more viewers interested. The more relevant tags you use, the more often your video will pop up when people search it. For example, if you're posting a video of your cute sleepy dog, you could use words like "Sleepy," "Dog," "Hilarious," and "Cutest." Make sure you don't include extra tags in the description, as those are not included when people search for them.

You can use tags that describe your video as well as other relevant popular videos to make sure that as many people as possible see your video when they are searching YouTube.

SHARING WISELY

Share your video with as many people as you can as soon as you post it. The earlier you share it, the more likely it will be to be a YouTube sensation. If you wait a week to share it while it barely gets any views, it'll be much more likely to be forgotten by the YouTube community. Remember, timing is everything. Think of when your audience is likely to watch your video and release right before then (evenings and weekends are a good suggestion).

Email your video to your friends, family, and coworkers. Create an email list consisting of the people who know you well enough to be actually intrigued by your new YouTube video, and send them the link and encourage them to watch it.
You can even add, "I can't wait to hear what you think!" to show that you really expect them to watch your video. If you don't care about potentially annoying people, just send it out to as many people as you can.

If you have an intriguing subject and a persuasive email, there's a good chance anyone will look at the video without even knowing you very well.

Share your video through social media. Post your video on Facebook, Twitter, and any other social networking sites that you've joined.

Use a blog or a website to promote your videos. If you have a blog or a website, you can use it to market your videos. If you don't have a blog or website of your own but know friends with websites or blogs that are popular, ask your friends if they can help you out by sharing your video with their fans.

EDITING

Take out white space. Create your video, then go into an editor and remove the long pauses, and other distractions in the video. If the video paces faster, people will continue to watch.

Add music to your Video. A good audio track can spruce up the video and disguise any audio problems you may have had. YouTube just released an audio library you can choose from.

Include text information – an email address, website, twitter handle and more. Some people may not be watching this video on YouTube. You want them to know who you are in those cases. Text can also keep or direct attention on-screen. Use it to your advantage.

Create credits (maybe some bloopers). Put something at the end of your videos to point where they can find you. Add some bloopers or extra footage. People love to see the extras at the end and your watch time might increase.

CHAPTER SEVEN

HOW TO USE YOUTUBE FEATURES TO PROFIT

What do all successful YouTubers have in common? They create great videos. But beyond that, smart video creators are using some of YouTube's tools and features to harness the power of those videos and their intended viewers. Have you optimised your channel?

Here is a simple checklist you can reference to make sure you are doing everything you can to boost views, build a loyal audience, and earn more money through YouTube.

HOW TO OPTIMISE YOUR YOUTUBE CHANNEL

Choose your channel name — the channel name is different from your channel URL, so you can edit this name. But it is best to pick a name and stick with it for consistent channel branding. Choose something that is short and memorable (like your band or artist name), and that lets viewers know what to expect from your channel.
Go here: https://www.youtube.com/account and click to edit on Google+.

2. **Choose your channel icon** — Upload a square, high-res (800×800) image that is recognisable and looks great when displayed at smaller resolutions (so use text sparingly). This image will be your channel's icon throughout all of YouTube.

   If you link your channel to G+, you can use an image you have previously uploaded to your G+ account.

   You can access this from your YouTube account page.

3. **Upload your channel art** — Channel art is the banner/header that appears towards the top of your channel when viewed on a desktop. Upload a large image (2560×1440) with the most important visual elements located in the inner 1546×423 area (so they will still appear when you scale the image for mobile and tablet). See the image below for various display dimensions.

   Make sure your channel art reflects your personality and does not just come off as some kind of boring brand logo. Check out YouTube's channel art tips and template here.

Dimensions for YouTube channel art

4.   **Write a channel description** — Move your cursor to the top right of the channel art section, and click "edit links." Be sure to highlight the most important content you create, use relevant keywords, and include your upload schedule to set expectations for your audience.

5.   Add website and social media links to the About tab — Corresponding icons will be displayed as overlays on your channel art. Include links to your official website, store or product page, social accounts, newsletter signup form, or promotional campaign pages.

Set "Featured Channels" — on the right hand side of your channel, you will see the "Featured Channels" header. Add any related or similar channels; including channels for other creative projects, you are involved in, your record label, etc.

7. **Enable browse view and discussion** — in the section of your YouTube channel homepage that contains the channel name and tab names, hover on your cursor in the right-hand corner until the pencil icon appears. Click "edit channel navigation" and then enable both the browse view and discussion settings.

8. **Select or upload a channel trailer** — once you enable the browse view, select a channel trailer video for your channel. A Channel trailer is a short video that will auto play whenever an unsubscribed viewer visits your channel, so here is your opportunity to get them hooked!

Your trailer should be informative and fit the overall vibe of your channel (oh, and did we mention it should be brief?). Also, you should ask viewers to subscribe. The trailer will automatically display a card at the end of the video giving viewers an easy way to subscribe.

9. Add sections to organise your channel —

Sections are a great way to organise videos (by theme, style, series, genre, etc.) and give viewers an easy way to explore your content from the Home/Browse page. Sections can consist of videos, playlists, or channels, and can include your own videos as well as content uploaded by other YouTube users.

For most viewers, only your top section will be visible without scrolling — so make sure you include your most important videos in the section at the top of your channel page. Also, because sections can contain content from other channels, you have a great opportunity to cross-promote with other artists and curate an interesting viewing experience for your audience. To add a section, just click the "Add a Section" button from the bottom of your channel home page.

10.   Customise your   channel url —
YouTube.com/MyName is a lot easier to remember than: YouTube.com/abcdefghijk123nnwwww.

Your channel must be at least 30 days old, have 500 subscribers, channel art, and a channel icon to access this feature.

Optimizing your YouTube channel with advanced features

Verify your YouTube channel — Go to http://www.youtube.com/account_features. If your account status has not already been verified, click "Verify" and select to verify by Voice Call or SMS.

Select your default video category — Go to http://www.youtube.com/account_defaults and change the category to the one that most closely reflects your type of channel, such as "music." You can always change these manually for each video once that video has been uploaded.

Compose a default footer for your video descriptions — Add links to your website and social media accounts as a standard footer in your default video description field. It'll your default video description field.

It'll save you lots of extra typing later on. To do so, go to:
http://www.youtube.com/account_defaults.

Again, you can always change these manually once a video is uploaded.

Add tags that will apply to most of your videos
— Tags help people find your video when searching on YouTube. Proper tagging can help increase monetization of your videos. Some suggested tags would include your artist name, any common misspellings, and popular keywords associated with your genre. Make sure tags with more than one word are enclosed in quotations, and don't use commas. Avoid overly generic tags or tags that are not relevant to your video. Create your default tags here http://www.youtube.com/account_defaults.

Grow your fanbase with Channel Ad, aka Fan Finder — With Fan Finder, YouTube will display your channel ad to viewers (as a skippable TrueView ad) at no cost to you — giving fans of other channels the chance to discover your videos!

To get started with a Channel Ad, go to https://www.youtube.com/featured_cont ent.

Click the button that says "select your channel ad" and choose a video to feature as your Fan Finder video. For tips on what makes a great Fan Finder video, visit http://www.youtube.com/yt/fanfinder/.

Feature a video or playlist with Featured Content (formerly know as "InVideo programming") — This feature allows you to highlight your most relevant content as an Annotation that appears when viewers watch your videos. To select content for InVideo programming, go to https://www.youtube.com/featured_content.

Add your logo as a watermark — This is another great branding opportunity, as your logo will appear in the lower right corner of your videos as a clickable link leading back to your channel page. To upload your logo, go to https://www.youtube.com/branding.

The image for the watermark should be a PNG or GIF file (1MB max) and ideally have a transparent background.

Add keywords for your channel – Many of these keywords will be the same or similar to your default video tags. That's ok. Use words that best describe the kind of content you are uploading to YouTube. To add keywords for your channel, go to https://www.youtube.com/advanced_settings.

Tell YouTube about your associated website —
What's your official website? You can help YouTube improve the quality of their search results by entering in that URL at https://www.youtube.com/advanced_settings.

Warning: it helps to have some familiarity with Google's Webmaster tool. If you're kinda new to all this stuff, associating your official website with your YouTube channel can be a little frustrating. But it's worth it. So keep trying, or just find an expert and ask for help.

Enable channel recommendations — This will allow YouTube to recommend your channel to viewers outside of your existing audience. To do so, go to https://www.youtube.com/advanced_settings. Include your Google Analytics property tracking ID — If you're already using Analytics, you can dive deeper into traffic stats by entering your Analytics ID into your YouTube account athttps://www.youtube.com/advanced_settings.

Allow advertisements on your videos — Go to https://www.youtube.com/advanced_settings and make sure to check the checkbox to allow ads.

Set your sharing preferences — Share, share, share! Go to https://www.youtube.com/account_sharing. Check your privacy settings — Modest? Go to https://www.youtube.com/account_privacy. Create your own compelling video thumbnail – The thumbnail is a quick snapshot that will represent your video on YouTube. In order to attract the most viewers, the thumbnail should be eye-catching. If your channel has been verified and is in good standing, you can (and should) upload your own custom image to make sure the thumbnail is as intriguing/exciting as possible. To upload your own custom thumbnail, click the "edit" button for the corresponding video in the Video Manager section of your account.

CHAPTER EIGHT

Why YouTube is Everyone's Favourite

Since the unveiling of Google's new Material Design language last year at Google's I/O event, there has been a progressive change in the look and feel of Google's software and services. Unlike Google's former design language, Holo, which was specifically created for Android, Google promised us that material design would be adopted across all of their offerings from Android, to Chrome OS, Android Wear, Android Auto, Android TV, and their web apps and services.

The announcement of material design embarked Google on the ambitious and painstaking journey to unify all of their disparate software under one cohesive banner. The most innovative aspect of material design is not simply its look and function. Although undoubtedly beautiful, material design's ability to be scaled across so many realms is its true crowning achievement. One year later, Google is still busily updating and refining their software to neatly fit into the material design language; unlike previous promises to improve the cohesiveness of Google's user experience the company is actually following through. The latest service to receive a make-over is the YouTube desktop player, which takes inspiration from the YouTube app. In typical Google fashion, they are selectively rolling out the new player to some users before a widespread launch.

The new player features transparent controls over the top of the video that disappear when inactive, much like the controls and progress bar found on mobile. These new controls annex the opaque black bar found underneath videos that we have grown used to for years (see gallery below).

The new design gives more space for the video to shine through, which is certainly a welcome improvement. The progress bar is now also thinner and expands to make seeking to a particular point in the video much easier; overall it looks much more modern and refined. Settings accessed via the cog in the lower right-hand corner, have also been updated (see gallery below).

Toggles for autoplay and annotations are now rounded to fit the material aesthetic, and speed and quality dropdown menus resemble their mobile counterparts. Another notable aspect of the new player is the omission of the "watch later" button from the player's controls, however, this feature is still accessible via the
"Add to" menu found above a video's description. While we can't say with confidence that the button is being removed because the new player is still in testing, Google's choice to test the service without the button is interesting regardless.

The color schemes of the icons and controls are much brighter and have greater contrast than the old player. Everything is bright white, red, and transparent black rather than the dull grays and red found on the previous version. The icons have also been redesigned with a modern, bolder look and appear to be slightly larger making them more prominent when active.

All said, the new player is much more appealing from a visual standpoint; it is far more vivid, clear, and refined. The way all the controls and menus appear to be floating give it a futuristic appeal, much like the floating action buttons prominently featured in material design. While we have no idea when the new player will be featured on a larger scale it is possible to try it out for yourself.

To do so you will have to change the value of the YouTube cookie VISITOR_INFO1_LIVE to Q06SngRDTGA. Chrome users can simply install the EditThisCookie extension from the Chrome Web Store in order to change this cookie's value. Make sure the English (US) interface is also enabled (accessible via the menu at the bottom of the settings page).

CHAPTER NINE

YouTube is A Delightsome Application

YouTube's office is filled with its history. Inside the San Bruno, California, headquarters, about 45 minutes from the Googleplex in Mountain View, there's a YouTube video on every screen. Over here, the Smarter EveryDay guys talk about the brain-bending backwards bicycle. Over there, Rick Astley promises he's never gonna let you down. (YouTube's employees work in a semi-permanent state of RickRoll.) On a table in one of the office's many kitchens, there's a pile of remotes for Google TV devices underneath a handwritten "FREE" sign. And of course, the red play button is everywhere you look: big doorways, small desk ornaments. The conference rooms are named after YouTube phenomena: Double Rainbow, It's a Trap, Dos Equis Guy, and on and on and on. Inside the Lolcats conference room, VP of product management Matthew Glotzbach is describing the future of YouTube. He envisions an app so good, an algorithm so perfect, that it knows exactly what you want to watch at any given time. You wake up in the morning and catch up on the news while you get ready. Then, throughout the day, YouTube shows you shorter videos when you're waiting in line or in the bathroom: maybe some gadget reviews, or the best Jimmy Fallon bit you missed last night. At night, you come home, and use Chrome cast to watch a movie or an episode of Video Game High School on your TV. YouTube wants to be more than a search engine for video. It wants to be the future, a perfect blend of TV and the internet, where everything is on demand but there's always something on.

A decade after its debut, YouTube is a behemoth. It's become the place for video online. Three hundred hours of video are uploaded every minute, and it has well over a billion users worldwide. It's spawned a crop of celebrities, real honest-to-goodness famous people.
It's by some measures the world's second-largest search engine. And it has pioneered entirely new ways of creating and consuming video. Video was ascendant in the last decade, and it's going to be inescapable in the next one.

YouTube can't relax, though. Not yet, not ever.
New challengers—everyone from Facebook and Snapchat to Vimeo and Vessel—are eyeing its talent and ready to poach its viewers. Absolutely everyone is coming for its advertisers, who have untold billions to spend and serious demands about where it goes. YouTube needs to prove it can turn impossibly huge view counts into actual, real profit.

The plan? Make sure everyone on the planet can get online, and on YouTube. They're working with carriers and ISPs to figure out how to stream to anyone no matter what their connection looks like. Then, get so good at showing them videos they like that they'll never want to turn off. That requires teaching their computers what's inside your videos, what videos you want to see, and what formats and video types are coming next. The video industry moves fast, and YouTube has to stay faster.
Simple, right?

33

Just Press Play

Buffering is the dirtiest word at YouTube. The people who work there say it a lot, always with a sort of cringing, pained look. It's like they're remembering a bad breakup or just woke up to a crushing hangover.

"There was some stat that we used to have that was like, if the YouTube buffer symbol was a webpage, it would be the third most popular website in the world," Glotzbach says. Then he hastily adds: "Not now, though!"

That's been the mission since even before Google bought YouTube. You've probably seen the first video, from January 2005, of "me at the zoo." This is YouTube's "just setting up my twttr" moment, and has become a key part of the mythology. You probably also remember the video a year later, when Chad Hurley and Steve Chen announced they'd sold to Google for $1.65 billion. YouTube grew furiously, giving people an easy way to upload and share video that previously would've resided only on Handycams and Mini-DVs, never to be seen by anyone. It wasn't complicated or powerful—that was the whole point. With Google, YouTube hit the big time. The acquisition was an obvious one; the two companies desperately needed each other.

"Google Books was going on at the time, ingesting all the books," says YouTube's VP of engineering John Harding, who was one of the first Google Video employees. "And we had said, what would it take to have all the video?" Google built the tech for Google Video, scaled it to infinity, and had absolutely no idea what to do with it. Meanwhile, Harding remembers,

"YouTube had a very fantastic user product." It made it easy for people to upload their own video, and its popularity exploded from the get-go. But YouTube didn't know how to scale; it was buckling under its own success. It was a perfect marriage, even if Google Video did live on in awkward redundancy for a few more years.

CHAPTER TEN

Reaching Millions through YouTube Videos

It wasn't that long ago that marketer thought they were hip to YouTube by posting their TV commercials to the site and eking out a few extra eyeballs. But with the potential now to reach millions and the popularity on social media of video stars like Michelle Phan, more than 150 brands have teamed with an array of talent on Google-owned YouTube and a handful of networks to produce entertaining and engaging ads.

"Creators on YouTube are increasingly crossing over into mainstream pop culture," said Jamie Byrne, YouTube's director of content commercialisation. "Most brands are looking at these collaborations as part of a larger campaign or media program."
Google upped the ante last year with Google Preferred, a program that allows advertisers to buy into the top 5 percent of lifestyle and entertainment video on the site, thereby guaranteeing that spots will appear across the most popular channels. The program, which will be promoted as part of Google's NewFronts presentation this week, has served marketers well, according to YouTube executives, with ads averaging an 80 percent increase in recall and brand awareness growing 17 percent. When Toyota wanted to put the redesign of its 2015 Camry to the test, the automaker enlisted comedy duo Rhett & Link to film crazy stunts— like a wild ride on a supercross track where they blew through a ring of fire.

"We felt like we had a unique message to tell and wanted to see how far we could extend that message," explained Florence Drakton, Toyota's manager of social media strategy and operations.

To further amplify the video's reach, Toyota ran ads using Google Preferred. While the two-minute clip generated a modest 74,000 views on Toyota's channel since being uploaded in November, Rhett & Link gave the Camry a shout-out during six episodes of their daily Good Mythical Morning YouTube talk show, bringing the total more than 10 million views.

Takeaway: Even big brands like Toyota can't bank on people finding and watching online commercials on their own. Plugging into the videos that influencers are already creating on a daily basis will be more effective, said Rhett & Link's Link Neal. "They're not expecting or desiring a commercial—they're desiring to be entertained by Rhett and me."

While Jennifer Lawrence did her part last fall to build buzz for The Hunger Games: Mockingjay – Part 1, Lionsgate also tapped five influencers for its "District Voices" YouTube campaign to rev up online chatter. Each social star was assigned a district portrayed in the film's fictionalized country of Panem. They were given props and costumes and tasked with producing original news stories that have a fan film vibe.

"We didn't want it to feel like we hired stars for any scripting," said Danielle DePalma, Lionsgate's evp of worldwide digital marketing and research. Lifecasting star Justine Ezarik, founder of iJustine, focused on District 6's transportation system, scoring nearly 400,000 views. And Jimmy Wong and Ashley Adams from the cooking channel Feast of Fiction made goat cheese tarts for District 9. Collectively, the five videos generated 2.5 million views without the aid of paid media.

Takeaway: Create fresh, original content that feels genuine and made by real fans.

Beauty blogger Eva Gutowski's shows fans of her MyLifeAsEva channel how she uses Proactiv as part of her morning routine in a goofy, relatable DIY video that picked up 385,000 views. "Eva really identified with the creative, which is often tough with brand-produced content," said Scott Fisher, partner and founder of Select Management Group, which manages Gutowski. And in a football-themed spot, Hudson Luthringshausen painted grease stripes under his eyes using a face mask.

All told, the 15-part series drove a 72 percent increase in subscribers, more than 2 million views and 13 million impressions. Proactiv continues to pour more investment into one-off

YouTube videos. "We can't just assume that what worked before is what's going to work in the future," said CMO Jay Sung. "We have to keep experimenting to try different messaging."

With bloggers rivaling magazine editors for power in the fashion world, Macy's partnered with style bloggers Claire Marshall, Jenn Im, Shameless Maya, P'Trique, Amy Pham and Claire Marshall, plus Maker Studios, to find the hottest new designer.

The retailer's eight-week "The Next Style Star" series pitted 16 designers against one another for a prize of $10,000, plus the chance to have their work displayed in Macy's flagship store in New York and style a photo shoot. In each episode, designers had 10 minutes to pull together a look using clothing and accessories from Macy's millennial-geared Impulse department. (Stylist Roman Sipe won with three different sweater looks.)

CHAPTER ELEVEN

How YouTube Dominated Online Video Sharing Platform after 10 years

Ten years ago, a 26 year-old Jawed Karim made a video of himself standing in front of some elephants at the San Diego Zoo. When the 19-second clip went live a few weeks later on a new video-sharing platform that he was testing, it set in motion a seismic shift in the way we consume and publish video content. That moment, YouTube was born.

According to Karim, the inspiration for creating YouTube came from two very different events in 2004: the Asian Tsunami and Janet Jackson's famous wardrobe malfunction at the Super Bowl half-time show.

Despite both events being extensively filmed and widely reported, Karim found locating the footage difficult. He raised the issue with two friends at a San Francisco dinner party and the three of them set about finding a solution. Fast forward to 2015, and YouTube – now owned by Google – is a very different platform. Today, it has over a billion monthly viewers and 300 hours of video are uploaded to the platform every minute.

YouTube is truly mobile, with over half of daily views coming from mobile devices. What the founders couldn't have predicted, though, is the way in which the consumption and creation of content on the platform has changed.

A decade on, YouTube is more than just a video hub: it is a place where people celebrate their passions, learn new skills and even start businesses. It is also a platform for artists, public figures, brands and individuals to reach vast, diverse and engaged audiences.

I'm often surprised by the variety of ways people tell me they use YouTube. In particular, people love to use it to learn new things: facts for an exam, knitting, folding up a buggy, fixing electronic devices, dancing, painting model figures, tying a tie and getting a six-pack.

Just the other week, I managed to fix my bike's front derailleur, thanks to a YouTube video on my phone. Videos in the "education" category on
YouTube are actually viewed twice as much as videos in the "pets and animals" category.
YouTube is also a place where we consume vast amounts of television content. With around 60 per cent of views occurring outside the original upload region, YouTube allows broadcasters to reach viewers on a global scale. New talent crops up on YouTube every day. For the advertising industry, YouTube has been revolutionary. For one thing, it allows brands to reach their consumers right at the moment they need or want something specific. If, as I was, you're searching for instructions on how to fix your bike, you might be in the market for a screwdriver, or a chain keeper. You might even want to buy a new bike.

On YouTube, brands can respond to this need and produce just the thing you're looking for, just when you want it.

Brands have also been quick to embrace YouTube as a creative platform, delivering breakthrough, iconic advertising moments which have become a part of culture and conversation. Remember the Old Spice campaign? Three's Dancing Ponies? Evian's
Babies?

When we first launched our skippable TrueView video ad format, we weren't sure if people would stay to watch the ad. But we found that when ads are as engaging as content, people will choose to watch them. In fact, last year four brands made it into the top 10 trending videos of the year. That's helping to make this incredible tool free for anyone to use.

So, what will the future bring? The truth is, we don't know. We don't know because where we go will be driven by the visions of our creators and the interests of our users. One thing we do know is that the world is coming online.
Currently, about three billion people have access to the Internet. By 2020, we estimate the figure will be five billion. That's five billion potential YouTube contributors and five billion potential viewers.

BONUS

Shoot your video and upload it, but only after creating a short, memorable title for it

Ensure you're signed up with an operational email address and wait for the elusive YouTube email stating you can apply for revenue sharing Install Google AdSense to your channel (you need to become a YouTube Partner before this but once you do, you can have ads on all of your videos)

Make sure to consistently upload great content to keep your audience engaged–you never know when your video could become the next viral sensation!

1. Advertise

Very first and important: You can do to make money from YouTube that by placing an advertisement on a video playing on YouTube. To advertise, YouTube offers to use Google AdSense. You can sign up with Google AdSense and start earning from your videos.

2. Affiliate Links

Making money from YouTube can also be done by creating an affiliate links posted below the video description. With this link you will get part of the profits from the sale of the video. Because, making selling video or number of view it is most likely link is clicked affiliates.

3. Pay per video review

Pay per video review is also one of the way to make money from YouTube. With these tips you can be active to offer the paid video to a potential target until the target has a substantial interest.

4. Promotion

This promotion can also help you to make money from YouTube to promote and send traffic to your website. With these promotions, you must be good at expressing your intent and convince the target to be more interested and are interested in pay-based promotions.

5. Sell Channels

One of the important and secret tips to make money from YouTube is that you can sell your channel with any one if you have many subscribers and likes. This can be done with expensive rates.

Summary

1.   Use YouTube to get traffic to your website and blog.

If you have a freelance website or blog which brings in income, you need traffic. Many websites were hard-hit by Google's Panda,

Penguin and Hummingbird updates. If this happened to you, you're hurting. You can use YouTube to not only regain traffic, but also increase it. Get started using the Creator

Playbook. Once you're set up, consider repurposing some older content into videos, as well as creating new videos. Make sure that you link to your own website in the first line of your video descriptions, so you can funnel your YouTube traffic to where you want it to go.

2.   Create products, do market research and promote them on YouTube.

If you're creating your own products or would like to, YouTube offers unlimited ways for you to promote your products and make sales.

Products you can create include eBooks, apps, art, and music. Create your products, and add them to a shopping cart. Then use YouTube to promote them. As we mentioned above, add a link to your product in your video's description, so that viewers can buy.

YouTube is an amazing resource for market research, too – you can soon discover whether your brilliant, innovative idea is likely to be profitable. For example, if you've got an idea for a product, but need funding, create some videos before you create a Kickstarter.com campaign. The views and comments on your videos will tell you whether your idea is viable in its present form. The YouTube audience can even help you to make it viable, so that your efforts to get funding are successful.

3. Sell others' products as an affiliate marketer.
"Affiliate marketing" means selling products in exchange for a commission. Hundreds of thousands of companies offer attractive deals to affiliate marketers who promote their

products, including huge companies, like Amazon and eBay, as well as smaller companies. Additionally, there are many affiliate networks you can join. These networks include Click-Bank, Commission Junction, and ShareASale.com.

To make money from YouTube as an affiliate marketer, review your affiliate products on video, or create "how to use this product" tutorials, don't forget to link to your products in your YouTube descriptions, make sure you're using your affiliate link, or you won't get credit for sales.

4. Get creative: Create a Web TV series.

Love telling stories? YouTube lets you create your own Web TV shows. You're limited only by your imagination... and your budget. You can create a comedy series, a drama series, or your own talk show. Be aware that YouTube limits your show's length to 15 minutes until you've become a partner. To upload longer videos, you'll need to increase your limit. If you're a frustrated filmmaker, TV producer or screenwriter, get a few friends together, and record your own TV shows. You never know. If you get lots of views, you may develop a new career.

5. Become a YouTube personality.

YouTube stars can make a lot of money. BlueXephos for example, has almost a billion channel views. At $7 per thousand video views, the income soon mounts up. If you've got quirky ideas, or are passionate about your interests but are camera shy? Get over your fears of being on camera and develop your YouTube channel! You never know, you may be the next YouTube star.

6. Monetize your videos with the YouTube Partner Program.

After you've created several videos, it's time to join the YouTube Partner Program. All you need to do is enable your channel for monetization, and you'll receive your share of the income from advertising on YouTube. Just as the YouTube stars do, you'll get paid for each thousand views on your videos.

7.   Teach: share your knowledge with tutorials.
Tutorials are huge on YouTube. If you know how to do something, you can teach others, and make money from your videos. Beauty and fashion videos are insanely popular.

8.   Become an expert on meta data: use keywords to get an audience and offer your expertise to others.
One hundred hours of video are uploaded to YouTube every MINUTE. This means that there's huge competition for attention. You need to do everything you can to ensure that your videos get found. Your videos' meta data will help. "Meta data" is data which gives information about your videos. In its Creator Playbook, YouTube tells you how to create your meta data:

YouTube is the world's second-largest search engine, and it uses metadata – your video's title, tags and description – to index your video correctly. To maximize your presence in search, promotion, suggested videos and ad-serving, make sure your meta data is well optimized.

Optimizing your videos for search makes the difference between success and failure, so be sure to do it. Once you get the hang of ranking YouTube videos well, you can search for hidden gems, really great videos not getting the attention or ranking they deserve, and offer your video optimization services to the creators. You could also create an online video series and sell access through YouTube's pay per view program, too.

9. Build your brand using YouTube.

As marketing guru Tom Peters pointed out way back in 1997, you're a brand, and you have power. YouTube helps you to amplify YOU.

Whatever you're doing, and whatever your job,

YouTube can help you to become known for your strengths, and make money. Even if you have no clear idea on how you could make money on YouTube, get started creating videos about your interests. You may just stumble across a gold mine… just as the people who turned their pets into stars have done.

10. Turn your child or pet into a star (and make money):

Two cats, Lil Bub and Grumpy Cat, started out on YouTube, and have become worldwide stars, with book details.

"You do not have to be a singer to become a YouTube star. If you are lucky, you could shoot a video of your child, pet, or a double rainbow that strikes a chord and goes viral." So keep your video camera handy or, better yet, learn to shoot great video with your mobile phone, which you'll probably have with you most of the time anyway. If you see something cute, video it, and upload the video. You never know who or what will be the next video sensation.
Create that sensation and you'll make money. So there you have it – ten creative ways video entrepreneurs can make money on YouTube! With hundreds of hours of video being uploaded to YouTube every single minute, video content is clearly not a passing fad and YouTube is only one way that we are using the power of video to build our own businesses! What are you waiting for? The time is NOW to become a video entrepreneur. Above all, remember that Rome wasn't built in a day and neither will your YouTube channel. Stay the course and reap the rewards down the line.

For more Books from the Author:
1. Love, Courtship and Marriage in Africa: https://www.amazon.com/dp/B0079JHLR0
2. How to possess the Land and Live in Abundance: https://www.amazon.com/dp/B006ZCC63Q
3. Best Romantic Love Poems and Lyrics: https://www.amazon.com/dp/B005QDT5TI
4. Public Speaking Genius in 10 Minutes: https://www.amazon.com/dp/B00FARD3Z2
5. Video Production and Marketing: https://www.amazon.com/dp/B00681DN1I
6. 65 Formulas to Woo Her Charmingly: https://www.amazon.com/dp/B007UOMTH6

www.ingramcontent.com/pod-product-compliance
Lightning Source LLC
Chambersburg PA
CBHW081314170526
45166CB00011B/3520